Sea Fever

a poetic journey

by

Melinda Rice

Finishing Line Press
Georgetown, Kentucky

Sea Fever

a poetic journey

Copyright © 2016 by Melinda Rice
ISBN 978-1-944899-26-4 First Edition
All rights reserved under International and Pan-American Copyright Conventions. No part of this book may be reproduced in any manner whatsoever without written permission from the publisher, except in the case of brief quotations embodied in critical articles and reviews.

Editor: Christen Kincaid

Cover Art: Melinda Rice

Author Photo: John Rice

Cover Design: Elizabeth Maines

Printed in the USA on acid-free paper.
Order online: www.finishinglinepress.com
　　　　　　also available on amazon.com

Author inquiries and mail orders:
Finishing Line Press
P. O. Box 1626
Georgetown, Kentucky 40324
U. S. A.

Table of Contents

Stranded in the High Mountain Desert

Sunday Morning 1

Capturing the Bay 2

It's hard to define 3

1959 4

Monster Waves 7

Social Norms at Steamer Lane 8

surf shaman 9

Timmy G Tells Me About His Day 10

When did Gidget give up the beach blanket 11

Wanted: Female Deck Hand 14

Bride at the Helm 15

Trolling for Salmon off Noyes Island 16

China Cove 18

Child's Play at Twenty-four 19

So Big 20

Different Ways to Catch Salmon 21

Rx: Santa Cruz 23

Aloe Vera 24

Trying to keep what I think I want 25

Buried Treasure 26

Stranded in the High Mountain Desert

A wave of oily asphalt fumes
washes over me
as I step from my air-conditioned car
into the hot September afternoon.
It appears I must chart a course
to get to the store, navigate
the patchwork of parking-lot
pavement where thick ropes
of fresh tar fill in the cracks.

Beefed-up pickups from
the drilling fields muscle their way
past pedestrians, belch their diesel fumes.
One is jacked so high its
running board stares me in the face,
another could use two spaces
for all the mud.

Inside, I grab a hand basket
and hope to make this quick.
I just might manage since
I don't know anyone anymore.
It's Jeff's day off in produce
and Kim no longer works in meat.
The customers own the pickups.

When I reach the register,
the checker doesn't call me by name,
has to ask if I prefer paper
or plastic, calls a manager
to approve my check.

I feel like a salmon far out at sea:
I've spent over half my life here;
it's time to go home.

I must go down to the seas again
John Masefield/Sea Fever

for Mom

Sunday Morning

Down along the cloudy shore
crisp colors
rise in the forming curl.
A delicate wash of aquamarine
dissolves into grey,
ephemeral as a Eucharist
on the tongue of an innocent.

Capturing the Bay

I

At dawn the bay looks like an unmade bed.
Someone shoved back the blue blankets
and crumpled the soft white eiderdown.

II

Morning sunlight—scattered across the bay
like tiny sequins—
shimmies to a ragtime breeze.

III

If I hadn't seen them
gleaming just below the surface at noon,
I wouldn't believe so many stars
tumbled into the bay last night.

IV

Afternoon and the glassy, sea-green
tumblers smash—
spilling their frothy ginger ale
onto the sandy floor.

V

Sunset brings out all kinds
of people. Come sit
with me on the bench and dabble
in the colors.

It's hard to define

the shore, where water
ends and land begins.

Down along the pocked black rocks
at low tide, seagrass lies lank,
tangled as bright green hair.
Anemones quake in pale purple
as we approach, squirt their anger.
Minnows seek safety in a hole.

During a winter storm,
this world remains
hidden below the surface
while up above, waves
claw at the cliff, fling
sand across the pavement,
block the roads. We

gather by the lighthouse,
marvel at the power and wonder
why
we want to define the shore.

1959

summer was Santa Cruz
cruising north from Fresno on 99
take a left just south of Chowchilla
a straight shot to the Bay
Monterrey for fog
Santa Cruz clears by noon

no AC, not then
open windows at 60
like a fan blasting
to cool the air, 105 degrees
of heat, retreat to the coast,
Mom and the kids

Dad left to work
till the weekend
joins us to cast for perch
from the pier, the old
cement boat at Sea Cliff,
bring home a bucketful
for dinner

afternoon begins
at noon, picnic lunch,
bunch of towels, a blanket
and an umbrella—
basket full of goodies
beach full of bodies

work our way from shallow
to midriff, who'll be first
to dive under the breaking
waves, ride the swell,
float so well in all that saltiness
Mom keeps an eye out

seagulls snitch chips
from the blanket
squawk when we return
dripping, throw ourselves
on the hot sand to tame
the goose bumps

blue skin, quivering chins
salty sea at 55, can't
survive that kind of cold
for long, who'll run up
to the store for pop?
hop over to the stairs

brush sand from soles
pull on flip-flops
(we called them zories then)
I poured water
on my brother in his sun-
crazed sleep—once

he rose, a fierce zombie,
grabbed my wrist,
threw me
into the tumbling surf—
the boxer barked
till someone threw a stick

don't do it, 'cause
he'll come back to you
and everyone will stare, glare
until you throw it again
to shut him up, throw it
back on the cliff, he'll

find it in the ice plant
that drapes itself down
to the concrete wall,
whose dog was he
anyhow? didn't matter

teeth stop chattering
hot sand and sun-
burn, when will you learn
to wear a T-shirt? vinegar
on your back tonight

after dinner
fog rolls in, long pants,
sweaters, a walk to Foster Freeze,
back at the house there's
no TV, morning comes early,
low tide at 6:00.

Monster Waves

Battleship grey,
the water bearing down on us.
The older child,   I
cry,   *Dive!*
Hands locked together
we plunge beneath the breaking wave.

Crush of ripping turbulence,
CO_2 tight in my chest,
a deadly urge to gulp
for air
as we hold on and then rise

to face another wicked wall, grab
a quick breath and dive
and rise and

dive

and rise and

dive again.

Surfers see them as a *set*,
a crazy kind of roller-coaster,
something to celebrate.

No matter how old I get,
when I'm out there,
I know it's me they're after.

Social Norms at Steamer Lane

The waves are wearing blue today.
They twirl their flounced skirts,
give the guys a quick peek,
dare them to come closer.

It's a calculated flirtation. Laws
of science come into play.
Sirens wail in the distant streets,
men coming to rescue
the boys who've gone too far.

surf shaman

you skip along the water

like Jesus on acid

an artisan carving liquid green

I've seen you dance with the almighty

breakers, plunge into space

slip through the eye of a needle

Timmy G Tells Me About His Day

I don't know why
I paddled back out
after that wave, the one
I had all to myself
where I made an eight-foot
late drop
right off the lip and kept on flying,
turned and carved
that beautiful green wall,
dragged my fingers
through all that power

that had been building for hundreds
of miles, felt it surge
through my body,
encase me in a perfect barrel
and shoot me out the tube.

I believe in quitting while I'm ahead,
but there I was
pulling myself back out
into the thick of things,
planning to vie for position once more
with men twenty years my junior,
flex my experience against
their youth. And I did it
again.

When did Gidget give up the beach blanket

and buy herself a board,
tuck the bikini into a wet suit
and paddle on out? It's a rough
crowd she's running with, shooting
the curl, ripping
waves. She's quick
to case the set, grab
the best wave and take off.
Look for her hot pink board
as she cuts
between stragglers
leaving them to wonder:
How did I miss that one?

Wanted: Female Deck Hand

We weren't mail-order
brides, more naïve
than that, lured to Alaska
by adventure, ending up
married to the sea.

Virgins all, we spent
our honeymoons
perplexed by the workings of
long poles that thrust themselves
out and away from the boat
dragging 50-lb. lead balls
on 7-strand stainless steel wire.

We learned how to bait
fish with florescent plastic squid,
hoochies, as bright and titillating
as a feather boa
that shimmied along
behind 12-inch flashers,

a chrome-plated striptease
no fish could ignore.

Bride at the Helm

They were waving at me,
out there on the empty ocean.
All men on deck, hands
held high above their heads, waving.
I'd never seen a halibut crew at work,
paying out fathoms of longline,
didn't know how it sinks
to be left on the ocean floor, sinks
like an anchor to the ocean floor.

Our troller, on the other hand,
never left its gear behind,
trailed dozens of leaders with
sparkling lures from four
lead-weighted stainless steel
lines. To hold our course
meant cutting across their stern.
The waving sank in.

Swinging the wheel, I
waved back,
headed in a new direction.

Trolling for Salmon off Noyes Island
(a young bride and her groom, 1973)

Nightmares
weren't allowed
when I was out there
night was too short

anyhow. We'd drop the anchor at eleven or so,
be up and going by four,
once beyond the protection of the point,
the sickness set in,

nausea at three knots,
back and forth along the drag,
follow the ledge twenty fathoms below,
keep the leads from hanging up.

Grey water, grey
water, grey water.
Stale air or
diesel fumes (if I opened the cockpit window).
The regular chug of the engine
like a metronome
marking time.

We worked
around the *Haystack*,
the locals' name for Shaft Rock.
The tide runs strong there.

You can't let the boredom
win or you'll find the boat
sliding sideways toward destruction.
Slam another eight-track
into the tape deck if your mind wanders off,
thinks of Stuart,
how he went overboard,
disappeared in Chattam Strait
last week.

China Cove

It wasn't until after
we dropped anchor
off Coronation Island
John consulted the <u>Coast Pilot</u>.
China Cove, "insecure."
According to the radio, winds were
forty knots. We were stuck, yet
couldn't stop

reading: When Alaska's canneries
first opened, Chinese came
north to process fish. Late September,
1908, *The Star of Bengal* filled
with over 100 workers and
2 million cans of salmon was being towed
south for winter. The tug captain
encountered foul weather near the foreboding
island, sought shelter in the closest nook,
lost control. He

cut them loose. Chinese
huddled below deck.
The hull broke apart on the rocky shoals.
Few survived. John closed the book,

tucked it in-
to the rack above the bed
where we would spend the night.

Child's Play at Twenty-four

A *harbor day*, so rough
you stay on anchor
in a secure cove, we chose
to head *inside*, behind
the barrier of islands
that created Sea Otter Sound.
It was calm there, but
the fish were few.
John could do the work
alone. I pretended
we were cruising,
put on my bikini, and
climbed up onto the flying bridge.

Heading up wind, the
boat protected me
from a chill breeze, captured
the heat of the rare sun.

And I lay like a child
on a terry towel
on the beaches of California.

So Big

I found the worry stone
on a harbor day, one of those
days I secretly looked forward to
when John decided it was too rough
to go out and we stayed
tucked back in the protected cove
hanging on the anchor. That day we
rowed the little safety skiff to shore
so I could see the waves, how big
they were, justify doing
what I'd rather do every day, not fish.

At the top of the island
looking down toward the *outside*,
I was disappointed. They
didn't look big. I couldn't see
their gaping maws, couldn't feel
the shudder, pitch, and roll
from a rush of grey water.

How big is worry?
About the size of a duck egg,
smooth and comfortable
in the palm of a sweaty hand.
I've laid it aside,
haven't picked it up in years.

Different Ways to Catch Salmon
2015

It says here they've got a resort
on Steamboat Bay, the *ultimate
luxury experience*. No reveille
at 4:00 a.m. to catch the morning bite.
No hurried oatmeal,
anchor chain, diesel exhaust.
Leave the tide books to the staff.
Let them find the fish. You're
encouraged to sleep in.

I remember pulling into the bay
after a 10-day trip to sell cohos,
buy some canned goods, take
a shower, get ice. Most often we'd
make the 3-hr. run to Craig
for the few extra cents
a pound and the luxury of a day off
to buy groceries. But if the fish
were really running,
we wouldn't take the time.

According to this brochure, the fish
are always running and after you've caught
a few, you can relax in the hot tub or
meet on the cedar deck for cocktails,
smoked salmon, pickled herring,
before your *six-course dinner*.
Pull up an Adirondack chair,
hand-crafted by local artisans, the
lodge is made of native timber. A
near-total absence of electronic amenities
should complete the sense of
wilderness for the CEO.

There won't be any old-timers
telling stories,
like the time we stood there with our
mouths open as that 40-pounder
slipped across the fishy floor
of the packing house before being weighed,
disappeared through the drain hole straight
down to the bay. Packer estimated him
at 32, wouldn't pay a cent more.

Rx: Santa Cruz

My prescription for Prozac
expired one morning while I
sat gabbing on the porch step.

Three little pills
lay forgotten in the bathroom cabinet.
I was peddling to the farmers market
a few blocks from home.

I filled my bag with
fresh fat strawberries,
leggy asparagus, homemade
pasta, sourdough bread—
grabbed five stems of purple iris,
tossed a dollar in the can,
sat down in a plastic chair.
Live music, bass fiddle and guitar,
male and female harmony,
a song about kisses, *besos*.

A profusion of flowers
spilled exotic fragrance,
fathers chased children,
caught them, swooped them
into the air. Mothers Day.

Come, the kids have dinner ready,
cracked crab. Aren't the iris
lovely in that vase? You sit here,
next to John. Cheers!
Don't you just love
a good pinot?

Aloe Vera

Here
I allow morning to creep,
am in no hurry,
contemplate sea wrack
and salt air,
the gentleness of fog.
I have no doubt the tide will change
and afternoon will tumble in
like a giant yellow beach ball.

Soon the sand
will be littered with color-
ful towels, umbrellas, low-slung chairs,
skinny legs, bare backs, bikinis,
the hopefulness of sun screen,
a crazy quilt of cocoa-butter tans.

Trying to keep what I think I want

would be like

pulling a starfish from a rock
and taking it home to dry in the sun,
tacking it to the bulletin board,

or boiling the pretty little olive shells
to make the crabs come out,
stringing a periwinkle necklace

it would be like a fish
forgotten in a bucket
left out in the heat,
you meant to put it back
but didn't.

Buried Treasure

The beach is full of rocks,
riprap so that
the best you can do at high tide
is watch from the cliff.

The stairs are still there,
pock-marked cement, slippery
from the comings and goings
of surfers, salt spray,
and whatever microorganisms
have chosen to take up residence.

I rarely bother to swing by
on my way to other beaches,
but yesterday I
descended the soppy steps
and picked my way
through the pile of ragged boulders
to the low-tide sand.

The reek of kelp was familiar
for a foggy morning, but what I sought
is getting harder to find. I'd need
the sun for starters to parch the . . .

Well, no,
first, remove the riprap,
shove the margins back
even further than the current
concrete wall, expose
the old one as rough as
the coarsest sandpaper, ice plant
dripping over the ledge.

Then the sun could come
with a smattering of children
hopping in *Mother-May-I* giant steps
across the sizzling surface
of a noonday beach, spilling
purple Shasta soda from already-
opened pop cans as they rush
to the safety of the shade
under Mom's umbrella.

And the cove would moderate
the breakers so at mid tide
it would be just right
for all those kids
now nagging their mothers
to let them go in, to forget
about the required hour of waiting
after gulping gritty sandwiches
and tossing the crust to the gulls.

When did Santa Cruz build the yacht harbor?
It must be over forty years ago
the giant breakwater
first disturbed the natural flow of sand.
That could well explain
why these memories have clouded
like beach glass, but who
can tell me why
I'm almost eager to let them slip
through my fingers like Mother's ashes
into the flooding tide?

ACKNOWLEDGMENTS

Thanks to the artistic community of Santa Cruz, Poetry Santa Cruz, and the gang at Marcia's house for inspiring me to write these poems to begin with, and to Sally Ashton for showing each of us how to create our own small collection. Your guidance during the early stages not only challenged me to improve my craft, but helped me envision a goal. Thanks to my critique group that met monthly in Grand Junction, CO. We called ourselves, "Waiting for the Swell." A black and white photo by the same name hung on the wall of the bagel shop where we met (yes, in Grand Junction, CO): a group of guys outside a surf shack in Santa Cruz, CA, 1940. You pushed me to the next level. Thanks to Jennifer Hancock for providing an even more-detailed editing when the collection was near completion. Thanks to Timmy G., the surf shaman, for pulling me into his surfing world. Thanks to John who introduced me to the fishing life and who was willing to leave it when I became desperate for sun.

Melinda Rice was born to sun in Fresno, CA. Nurtured on nursery rhymes and the lyrical language of the King James translation of the Bible, she grew to love words at an early age, especially reading, writing, and reciting poetry. Melinda graduated from the University of North Dakota with a degree in elementary education. In 1972, her search for a teaching job combined with a wanderlust and a love of dramatic natural settings led her to Southeast Alaska. There she taught fifth grade and met her husband John. During the summers she joined him to fish commercially for salmon off the coast of Noyes Island. Eventually, the gloominess of the SE Alaskan climate and the sickness brought on by rough seas outweighed the adventure. She was ready to move back south. In 1978 Melinda and John found a beautiful piece of land on the Western Slope of Colorado where they built their home and raised their family. Except for a few years fulltime in Santa Cruz in the early 2000's, they have lived on 6 acres outside Parachute, Colorado. They make regular trips to both California and Alaska.

www.ingramcontent.com/pod-product-compliance
Lightning Source LLC
Chambersburg PA
CBHW060225050426
42446CB00013B/3170